DAMN YOU, AUTOCORRECT!

Hilarious text messages you didn't mean to send

Jillian Madison

7 9 10 8 6

Published in 2011 by Virgin Books, an imprint of Ebury Publishing
A Random House Group Company

Copyright © Jillian Smith 2011

Jillian Smith has asserted her right under the Copyright, Designs and Patents
Act 1988 to be identified as the author of this work.

Every reasonable effort has been made to contact copyright holders of
material reproduced in this book. If any have inadvertently been
overlooked, the publishers would be glad to hear from them and make good in
future editions any errors or omissions brought to their attention.

The Random House Group Limited Reg. No. 954009
Addresses for companies within the Random House Group can be found at
www.randomhouse.co.uk

A CIP catalogue record for this book is available from the British Library

The Random House Group Limited supports The Forest Stewardship Council
(FSC®), the leading international forest certification organisation. Our books
carrying the FSC label are printed on FSC® certified paper. FSC is the only
forest certification scheme endorsed by the leading environmental
organisations, including Greenpeace. Our paper procurement
policy can be found at www.randomhouse.co.uk/environment

Design by Sunil Manchikanti

Printed and bound by the MPG Books Group

ISBN 9780753540084

To buy books by your favourite authors and register for offers visit
www.eburypublishing.co.uk

Dedications

To Mom & Dad.
Thank you for not owning smartphones, and for
only mildly freaking out when I shunned corporate
life to "work on the internets."

To Michelle.
Get ready, because tonight, we're goin' TOMCAT.

To Brie.
My best friend, and the most amazing
woodchuck you will ever meet.
I meant woman! Damn you, Autocorrect!

And to everyone who contributed to the website and this book.
Thank you for not proofreading before hitting send.
Text on, motherduckers!

Contents

Introduction

"DAMN YOU, AUTOCORRECT!"

If you own a smartphone, there's a good chance you've screamed that phrase at least once. Maybe you sent a text to your spouse that you "f'd the dog" (fed) or fired off a note to a co-worker about your "bad case of the manboobs" (Mondays). Either way, Autocorrect was likely the culprit.

While the feature on our mobile devices can be a blessing, it's also often a curse. It frequently changes words without rhyme or reason, and if you hit "send" too quickly, it can lead to some funny, confusing, or just plain embarrassing results. I found that out the hard way in the summer of 2010 when I innocently tried to invite a few friends over for an evening of gelato. My iPhone's Autocorrect, however, had another idea and asked them over for a night of "fellatio." And just like that, Autocorrect turned me into a hussy. What would my mother say!

Shortly after the gelato/fellatio incident, I started wondering if other people out there were having similar experiences with their smartphones. So I purchased the www.damnyouautocorrect.com domain, set up the site on a whim, and added about fifteen Autocorrect incidents involving myself and my friends. I could never have anticipated the public's reaction. As it turned out, there were millions of people who were just as frustrated by Autocorrect as I was.

By the end of its first week online, DamnYouAutoCorrect .com earned write-ups on ABC, CNN, Gizmodo, Mashable, *The Huffington Post*, and in dozens of other national media outlets. It went viral on Twitter and Facebook and, literally overnight, found itself getting over 1 million page views and five hundred submissions per day from people all over the globe. Those numbers have been steadily increasing every week.

I think DamnYouAutocorrect.com immediately struck a chord because people of every age can relate to it. These days, everyone texts, and the content highlights situations we've all been in ourselves. And even if we haven't, it's just human nature to enjoy voyeuristically peering in on the hilarious—and often cringe-worthy—text fails our peers have experienced.

And there have been some real doozies. This book is packed with three hundred hilarious images—most of which are found for the first time here—that highlight the unintentional hilarity that often ensues when Autocorrect goes wrong. These laugh-out-loud funny examples include:

- Co-workers talking about their "ejaculation" reports (escalation);
- A husband texting his wife that he "laid" the baby-sitter (paid);
- A cook warning someone not to touch a bowl of "masturbating" cherries (macerating);
- And of course, friends complaining about how much they hate the dreaded "auto erection" feature on their smartphone.

And then there's the most popular image on the DamnYou-AutoCorrect.com website to date: a father texting his daughter that he and his mother were going to divorce, when they were in fact just going to *Disney*. Oops! I'll take "texts I wouldn't want to receive" for $200 please, Alex.

BUT WHAT IS AUTOCORRECT, ANYWAY?

Autocorrect is a software function—commonly found on many smartphones and portable web-ready devices like the iPod Touch—that attempts to correct common typos on the fly by guessing the word you were really trying to write. In theory, Autocorrect's ultimate goal is to save time by automating spell check functions and offering predictions, often before you've even finished typing the entire word. But is this feature really improving our modern, super-connected lives?

We move fast, talk fast, and type fast, and there's no denying Autocorrect can be a huge help in certain circumstances. It often works as the silent hero in the background, making otherwise illegible sentences like "Ehag timr is yge mewtigg" show up properly as: "What time is the meeting?"

But not so fast! Unlike Jennifer Aniston's hair, Autocorrect isn't always perfect. It has a sinister side too—one that steps in and inserts completely inappropriate words that can make you look like an idiot, a creep, or (gasp!) a total pervert. The iPhone, for example, frequently autocorrects "Whitehouse" to "whorehouse" and "homie" to "homoerotic." If you hit "send" without carefully proofreading, the conversation will certainly take an interesting turn. And so might your evening.

OKAY, SO HOW DOES
AUTOCORRECT WORK?

As it stands right now, it's almost impossible to find information about exactly how the elusive Autocorrect feature works. It's a closely guarded trade secret among the mobile phone companies and software developers, and most of them are incredibly tight-lipped when it comes to discussing it.

What we do know is that when you start typing a word, the Autocorrect software checks those letters against a built-in dictionary. If it doesn't find an exact match, it guesses what you were trying to type and offers that word up as a suggestion. Many smart phones also have some sort of "learning" element as well, meaning they add new words and terms to the dictionary based on the user's behaviors and patterns of use. As a result, after a period of acclimation, no two Autocorrect dictionaries may ever be alike. That means if you're frequently using words like "anal" or "vagina," there may be an increased risk of your Autocorrect, uh, slipping those words in during future conversations. Sexters, beware!

HOW CAN THINGS GO
SO WRONG?

Autocorrect seemingly has a mind of its own—and as you'll see in this book, often a hilariously *dirty* one. The real trouble comes when you hit "send" without realizing the word you thought you typed was swapped out for something else. For me, there are two fundamental problems with the way the feature works on the device:

First, when you're typing, you're instinctively looking down at the keypad. The autocorrected suggestions, however, show up in the message area, making them incredibly easy to miss if you're typing quickly and not paying close attention. Second, when typing, all you have to do to accept the word suggestion is tap the space bar. That's it! The only way to get rid of the Autocorrect suggestion is to keep typing more letters, or to hit the little "x" next to the suggested word in the bubble. That's just not intuitive at all. Often, you think you're ignoring the word suggestion by just hitting "space" and continuing to type your message. But you've done just the opposite. The rest, as they say, is history. You've just been "Autocorrected," my friend!

HOLY MOLYBDENUM!
THAT'S TOTALLY HOOSEGOW!

DamnYouAutoCorrect.com receives about six hundred new submissions per day from the website and the iPhone/iPod Touch app, and I read every one of them myself to determine if they're website-worthy (hey, it's a hilarious job, but somebody's gotta do it). I've noticed several trends by doing all that reading, one of which is the relatively new "extra letters" phenomenon, in which the more you repeat the letter, the more strongly you mean it. For example, people frequently write the phrase: "let's gooooooooooooo!" Autocorrect dictionaries have no clue how to handle all those extra letters, and on the iPhone, it's often autocorrected to "let's hookup" or "let's hippopotamus"—either one of which might be incredibly embarrassing, especially if you're talking to a relative or a zookeeper. But that's a topic for another book.

Smartphones also love to insert nonsensical, totally random words that have absolutely nothing to do with what you're talking about. Did someone say something funny? Be careful when replying back with "hahahaha," because it's often autocorrected to "Shabaka"—an Egyptian pharaoh back in 700 BC. The word "hilarious" often gets autocorrected to "hoosegow"—a slang term for a prison. And for all my science geeks in the house (holler!), try typing "holy moly" into your phone. On my device, I end up with "holy molybdenum," the chemical element with the atomic number 42. But I'm sure you already knew that.

Science not your thing? Are you more of a sports buff? Just make sure you double-check your messages before you hit "send" on your iPhone, or you might find yourself talking about Derek Heterosexual (Jeter), Juan Urine (Uribe), or the great play you just saw the Boners (Niners) complete. Take my word for it—your friends will never let you live it down.

Many devices really seem to struggle with pop culture references too. For example, I use Twitter all the time, and no matter how many times I hit that little "x" to dismiss the suggested word, my iPhone tries to change the word "tweeting" (the process of sending Twitter messages) to "teething" and the word "retweet" to "retarded." Try explaining *that* one to your unsuspecting friends and followers.

Based on my observations with Autocorrect and the submissions sent into DamnYouAutoCorrect.com, these are the top twenty-five most common Autocorrect mishaps:

Word / phrase you're trying to write	Autocorrected to
Hell	He'll
A sec	Asexual or a sex
Awwwww	Sewers
Thing	Thong
Bitch	Birch
Give me a call	Give me anal
Oooohhh	Pooping
Grrr	Ferret
Whenever	Wieners
Pick me up	Oil me up
Keys	Jews
Shit	Shot
Coworkers	Visigoths or Coriander
Goooooo	Hookup
Fucking	Ducking
Hahahaha	Shabaka
Homie	Homoerotic
Sodium	Sodomy
Mani/Pedi	Mani/Penis
Pen	Penis
Yesyes	Testes
Soonish	Zionism
Netflix	Negroid
Kids	LSD
Parents	Parrots

Another thing that drives people "ducking" nuts about the iPhone—and a trend you may have noticed in the above list—is its almost comical aversion to swearing. It hates curse words, and does everything in its "ducking" power to prevent you from using them. It even goes so far as to insert an apostrophe in the word HELL (HE'LL), which obviously makes the word take on an entirely different meaning. Its desire to keep things PG-13 is often infuriating, because let's face it: Sometimes you just need to call someone a fucking asshole.

So now that you know what Autocorrect is and how it works, you're ready to get to the submissions. Just remember: If you don't want to end up like one of the poor motherduckers in this book, type carefully and proofread your messages . . . or you too might one day find yourself screaming: "DAMN YOU, AUTO-CORRECT!"

Peace out, homoerotic! And if you don't like this book, you can go to he'll! Shabaka!

1

Parents Just Don't Understand:

Awkward Texts with Mom & Dad

The Big "D"

Mom's Office Fight

 Messages **Mom** **Edit**

> i just got in a huge fight with a co worker

>> Why? What happened? Are you ok?

> stupid really... i needed a penis and he wouldn't let me borrow one

>> What???!!!??!

> oh I'm going to throw this stupid phone in the trash. I needed a pen.

 Send

12

Do Ducks Have Jackets?

Hot for Teacher

Way TMI for Dad

Messages **Daddy** Edit

You working today if you are can one of you p/u my meds

Yes and yes. How are you feeling today? ;)

Good how about you guys did you go to another bar

Yes but not for long. I think I'm getting dick. My throat hurts :(

Sick. Wow sorry daddy. My phone did that.

Send

16

Girls' Night

PARENTS JUST DON'T UNDERSTAND

Happy Birthday, Mom

Messages from Beyond

Shopping for Dad

Dinner Options

 📶 🔋 ⏰ **1:38** AM

...needs info about your school books.
Wed, Oct 13, 2010, 7:09 PM

Thu, Oct 14, 2010

 Mom: U desire which day it coming home? Was thinking of vagina chicken for dinner tonite...
Thu, Oct 14, 2010, 12:21 PM

Me: Reread that text
Thu, Oct 14, 2010, 12:24 PM

 Mom: Whoops...! Did u get a good laugh out of it?and did u understand what I meant?
Thu, Oct 14, 2010, 12:26 PM

Me: Yes, and so did everyone else in the lobby. And I have no idea what you meant
Thu, Oct 14, 2010, 12:27 PM

Sat, Oct 16, 2010

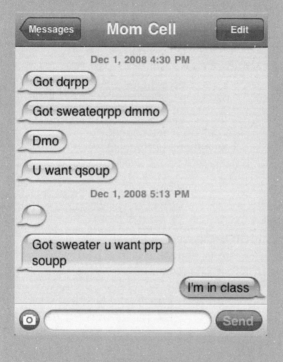

We've All Been There

Dec 1, 2008 4:30 PM

Got dqrpp

Got sweateqrpp dmmo

Dmo

U want qsoup

Dec 1, 2008 5:13 PM

Got sweater u want prp soupp

I'm in class

PARENTS JUST DON'T UNDERSTAND

Where's Dad?

Moms Cell

> Is dad around? I have a question about computers

He's getting a sex change but he left an hour ago so he should be back soon!

> A sex change?! Wow, in an hour, that's impressive

Oh for heaven's sake. I wrote oil change and this phone changed it.

> Thank god! Ok have him call me. Love you

 Send

DAMN YOU, AUTOCORRECT!

24

PARENTS JUST DON'T UNDERSTAND

Chores

Vacuum?

2010-12-15 3:45 PM

I will after homework.

Sounds good. U r awesome kid!

2010-12-15 5:57 PM

Gotta get cat food

Did u get to vexing

Caving

Vacuum

Caving? That sounds dangerous.

Send

DAMN YOU, AUTOCORRECT!

26

Accidental Insult

Finals Week

Mom

Hi, How are finals going?

Almost done. My testes have been really hard this semester.

I mean my tests!

Maybe you can talk to your father about that. Ha ha.

My testes are fine. My economics grade is another story

 Send

DAMN YOU, AUTOCORRECT!

28

Chew on This

Mom Cell

> Mom do you have any gum?

Yes I have a pack of juicy fruit in my puss.

> Whatttttttt?

In my puss

Puss

> Ew. I don't think I want that.

Purse damn it. New pack

Robot Invasion

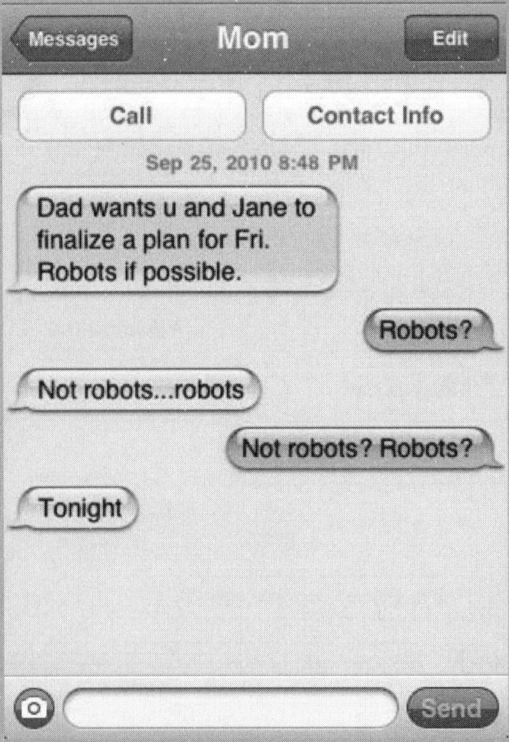

Under the Weather

PARENTS JUST DON'T UNDERSTAND

Thanksgiving Prep Work

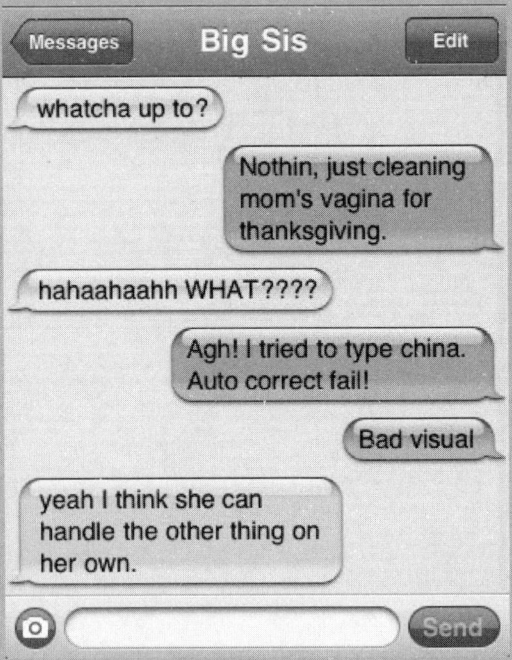

Day at the Salon

> On my way. Leaving the hairdresser's now.

Okay! How'd it go?

> Great! I got a blow job at the last minute.

> *out! A blow OUT!!! Not the other thing.

I didn't know they offered that service. Ha ha.

📷 ▢   Send

PARENTS JUST DON'T UNDERSTAND

DAMN YOU, AUTOCORRECT!

Is Mom Okay?

Arts & Crafts

Its better if the ribbon has wire on both side its easy to work with and holds its shape

I think both of mine do

Dec 21, 2010 11:12 PM

Can we do the boys Thursday morning-ish?

Bows* haha

What do the boys look like?...lol....Thursday will be fine for the bows....Iam to oid and to tired for the boys...haha

DAMN YOU, AUTOCORRECT!

Time Off

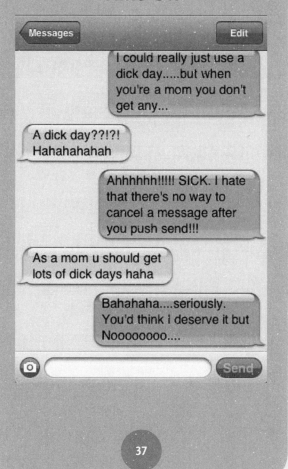

PARENTS JUST DON'T UNDERSTAND

DAMN YOU, AUTOCORRECT!

Return to Sender

PARENTS JUST DON'T UNDERSTAND

Ready, Freddie

Dad's Wish List

I need Christmas and St. Nick ideas for you ASAP!

Rihanna for my bald spot, filter for my craftsman 6 gallon wet/ dry vac- more to come.

Rihanna?

That is rogaine.

Lol

That would probably make me forget about my bald spot.

Ha ha

PARENTS JUST DON'T UNDERSTAND

Duck Hunting

Messages · Mommy · Edit

When u coming home dads duck hunting and taylors cranky

Why is he dick hunting it's dark

Using auto correct r we

It wasnt dark at 430 and its probably better to dick hunt after so no one will recognize u

Checking In

Messages · Mom · Edit

How were your teats?

My teats are fine thank you for asking

Haha glad your teats are fine

DAMN YOU, AUTOCORRECT!

Gee, Thanks

Very Dirty Harry

44

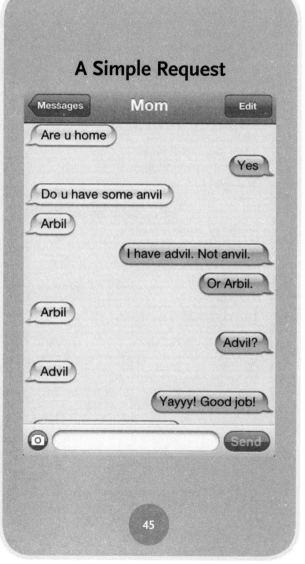

A Simple Request

Messages | Mom | Edit

Are u home

Yes

Do u have some anvil

Arbil

I have advil. Not anvil.

Or Arbil.

Arbil

Advil?

Advil

Yayyy! Good job!

House Sitting

Messages **Mommy** Edit

I am on vacation so we will come tomorrow. Water the panties please and I will tomorrow.

> Lol I'll water the panties

It won't let me say it right!!!

> Hahaha

Love you. Don't work too hard.

Send

DAMN YOU, AUTOCORRECT!

46

Job Options

Mom

She has no real leads right now and still can't even clearly define/figure out what she wants to do. She's torn btwn trying to find a real job and just pursuing temp work...

I am so incredibly sad for her.

I'll call her later xxxx

Thanks mom.

Perdue temp work

Like at a chicken farm?

PARENTS JUST DON'T UNDERSTAND

Ho-Ho-Horrible

Messages | Mom | Edit

Zantac in the neighborhood

Um

Santa

Hahaha

Dinner Plans

Messages | Dad | Edit

Kay either amicis or kapps?

How 'bout that Italian place where you got dick years ago?

...what......

Nov 13, 2010 7:32 PM

In for a Visit

When Dads Shop...

Fourth of July

> In the shuttle. Do u have tomorrow off? Fireworks don't start til 9 pm. I thnk Dad may be too tired. We went to East beach once and sat on the dick. Nice

> You said dick. Not deck. Nice

> Hmmm guess my proofreading days are behind me. Blame the

PARENTS JUST DON'T UNDERSTAND

Jeez, Mom!

DAMN YOU, AUTOCORRECT!

Congrats—Love Dad

Should FWD. Good news on UVM - Congrats.

Love. DAD

Sewer

Sweat*

Sewer

Sewer

OMG sewers

Ffffffff I am trying to say Awwwww

HOLY GOD

PARENTS JUST DON'T UNDERSTAND

Fourth Time's the Charm

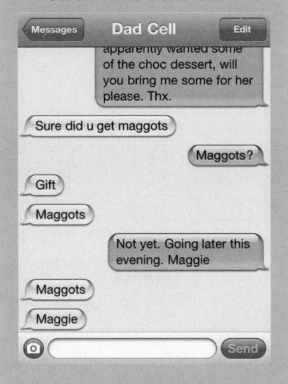

PARENTS JUST DON'T UNDERSTAND

Christmas Presents

Messages | **Mom Cell** | Edit

> Merry Christmas mom!

You too honey!

Did you get a lot of gonorrhea from Santa?

> What?!

Oh this darn phone/ did you get a lot of goodies from Santa I meant

> Lol yea I did! I must have been a good girl this year.

Send

2

Love Gone Wrong:

When Couples Text

Autocorrect & Relationship Advice Don't Mix

Messages **Amanda** Edit

Call | Contact Info

12 Nov 2010 15:15

> Don't worry, seriously. He's crazy about you and he loves you so much. He told me the other day that you're the first girl he had ever thought about the führer with. Xx

WTF?

> Ok so that was supposed to say future... Damn Phone! Xx

Send

Arguing Over Text

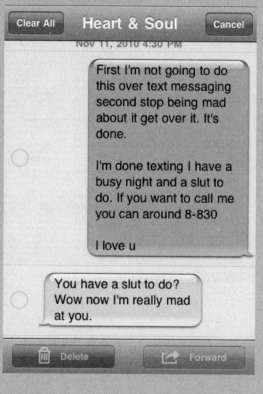

Clear All | **Heart & Soul** | Cancel

Nov 11, 2010 4:30 PM

First I'm not going to do this over text messaging second stop being mad about it get over it. It's done.

I'm done texting I have a busy night and a slut to do. If you want to call me you can around 8-830

I love u

You have a slut to do? Wow now I'm really mad at you.

Delete | Forward

Sexting Gone Wrong

Messages | Edit

Dec 24, 2010 2:05 AM

Sext me. Right now

Ohhhh baguette

Hahahahahahah

Babyyyyy*

Send

Terms of Endearment

Messages | **Michelle** | Edit

How's your book huni bunions

Bunions???

Lol. Oops. Huni buni*

Send

DAMN YOU, AUTOCORRECT!

62

LOVE GONE WRONG

A Night Apart

I'm home safely! I hope you got your key situation worked out. love you!! miss you tons already :)

Yay I'm glad!! :) I miss you tooo! Cockfight

cock fight?

Hahahaha it was supposed to be xoxoxoxo

I like cock fight better.

Haha okay :) I'm seriously busting up laughing

Send

The Babysitter

John

Did you guys eat dinner yet?

Yep. Just had pasta.

Oh by the way, I laid the babysitter.

Uh, excuse me? You fucking what?????

Hahah PAID. I paid her. Sorry to give you a heart attack babe.

I hate you! lol

LOVE GONE WRONG

Secret's Out

> Ahh we left the condom unwrapped in the garage lol I'm embarrassedd

> *garbageee damn auto correct!

Date Night

> I'm super pumped abt sharing a romantic stroke with you tonight!

> Omg! Stroll! Not stroke!! Oh dear god. I'm a pervert

Bahahahahahah

LOVE GONE WRONG

A Night In

You betadddddd!

that makes no sense

Haha I know. Leaving for your house in 2

Then we get to handcuff and cuddle!

???

Hangout!

that was kinky

...and I liked it;)

Hidden Desires

Hey! Around what time will you be here?

Mornin baby! I'm just leavin my place now so... About 15 mins.

Ok! Are you hungry? Cuz i really want a baby!

A baby? Dear god please tell me that was auto correct

Hahahahahah. I meant a bagel. Not a baby. Well maybe someday

Send

69

LOVE GONE WRONG

Do I Need to Be Worried?

Kiel

Mwah

I really want to kill u and lay on u

Lmao

Kiss

Hahahaha Omg

Lol i cant stop cracking up

I'm crying

The Crush

LOVE GONE WRONG

Drunk Dialing

DAMN YOU, AUTOCORRECT!

The Mall & More

I need to go to the mall but my sis has the car. Can u take me babe?

Yea I wanna go buy a game anyway. I'll oil your ass up in 45 mins!

Lol I wrote pick you up. In 45.

Good bc there will be no oiling of my ass in 45 mins or ever! Xo

Send

LOVE GONE WRONG

Bedtime Wishes

Grocery Shopping

Be home soon. Do you want anything from whore foods?

If you're at whore foods I'll take something tall and blonde.

But if you're at whole foods I'll take some peanut butter.

LOVE GONE WRONG

A New Measure of Time

Talia

I love you!!!!!!

I get to see you in 20 minidresses!!!!!!

Hahaha. Or minutesssss. I'll settle for either ;-)

Hahahahahahahahahaha hahahaha that's an amazing auto-correct error!

Autocorrect for the win!!!

Backhanded Compliment

LOVE GONE WRONG

Cure for the Common Cold

> Feeling any better yet honey?

I feel worse. I have a fever and I'm coughing and I can't breathe well. This totally sucks.

> Okay. I'm leaving work now. I'm going to bring you chicken soup and rub cocks on your chest.

Whattttt? Um I hope that was an autocorrect. I'm not that sick, babe :)

> Ahahahahaha. Vicks!!! Vapor rub to help your breathing. Laughing.

       Send

Bad Kissers

He kissed me. :)

Fun :-) was it good?

It was. But very different. He pushed the limits a bit but was respectful when I moved his hands. He is kind of a forceful kisser.

Inbreeding

Lol. That's terrible!

Tried to write "interesting" stupid autocorrect

Send

LOVE GONE WRONG

Surprise!

> We have 7pm reservations, where the heck are you?!

Sorry... Running a few mins late! I'll be lesbian in five mins, I swear.

> You're a lesbian now? Wish you told me that before we got married :)

Omg! I wrote leaving! I haven't been a lesbian since college. Kidding!

> Well get your ass here. I'm hungry!

DAMN YOU, AUTOCORRECT!

Nighty Night

LOVE GONE WRONG

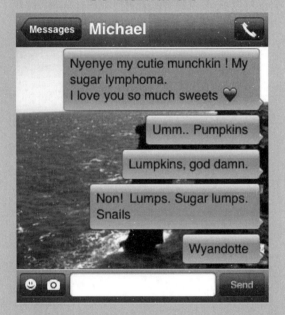

So Romantic

Messages **Michael**

Nyenye my cutie munchkin ! My sugar lymphoma.
I love you so much sweets 🖤

Umm.. Pumpkins

Lumpkins, god damn.

Non! Lumps. Sugar lumps. Snails

Wyandotte

Send

Living Together

Apr 18, 2009 6:21 PM

I'm home and I love u

Awww I'm looking for cute thugs to put in our apartment

Things??? I want to keep the thugs out

Unless you think they're decorative

I Love You THIS MUCH

Laur

and everything

22 Nov 2010 21:39

Did I mention I love you? I'm going to assign you your own dungeons.

Ringtone. Not dungeon.

DAMN YOU, AUTOCORRECT!

3

What's Cookin':

Autocorrected Food & Beverage Texts

Don't Touch the Bowl!

Messages
Edit

When you get home please do not touch the bowl on the counter!

Um, whyyyy?

There are cherries in the bowl And it's essential they not be moved. They're masturbating.

Whoa. I won't be touching anything that's "masturbating"

Send

WHAT'S COOKIN'

Special Dinner

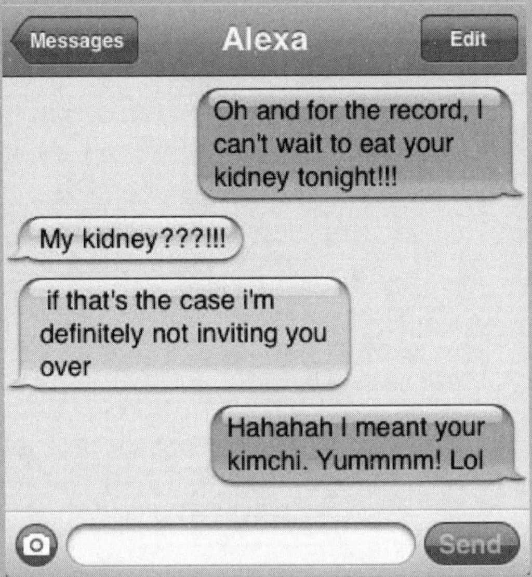

Anniversary Meal

happy anniversary hon! i will be cooking you boogers tonight!

Uh thanks but I had a late lunch :/

GAH! Bucatini! lmao

lol. Much better. I love you, but not enough to eat boogers.

  Send

89

WHAT'S COOKIN'

Bomb Squad

Can you please take out the hamburger to thaw out. I'm going to make spaghetti tonight.

Dec 14, 2010 12:22 PM

Did you set out hamburger for tonight?

Dec 14, 2010 1:44 PM

Hello?? You there??

Dec 14, 2010 2:31 PM

Hamburger is detonated

Dec 14, 2010 3:09 PM

What??

Lol not frozen

  Send

DAMN YOU, AUTOCORRECT!

Trader Joe's

> Trader Joes has some yummy stuff like gorgonzola stuffed croissants

> There's always miserable sticks, or egg rolls

> Lol! Miserable sticks!!!!

They sound fabulous. Do I fry them?
Ooh.
Was gonna ask..

> That was supposed to say mozerella sticks!

WHAT'S COOKIN'

Mom Loves Mexican

DAMN YOU, AUTOCORRECT!

Rosemary and Rhyme

> Can u start chopping some Rosemary and rhyme?

You want me to rhyme while i chop? Lol

> Lol

> Aint no stoppin / only choppin

Cuttin up myself some rosemary/betta wach my fingaz or its gonna get scary

Send

WHAT'S COOKIN'

Dinner at the Office

Hi hon, gotta work late tonight so will be home around 7

Ok, you gonna want dinner or are you grabbing something at the office

Depends! Did you cook?

Cooking now. Roast cyborg, mashed potatoes

In that case I'll eat at the office! :)

Haha chicken, you wise ass!

DAMN YOU, AUTOCORRECT!

94

Eating Out

Messages Edit

dude, wanna eat pizza sluts tonight?

Tonight tomorrow and every night

LOL. I meant pizza hut you perve.

📷 ⟨ ⟩ Send

Yum-O

Messages Edit

what r u doing

Watching rachael ray and eating a slave

Really? how's that taste?

Needs salt, you wise ass! I wrote salad. Damn auto correct.

📷 ⟨ ⟩ Send

WHAT'S COOKIN'

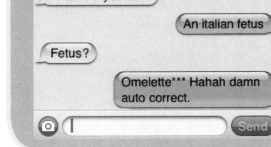

Romantic Dinner

> I'm making you dinner tonight

Is that so!

> Yep! And you're gonna love my chicken flatulence.

> Oh god oh god oh god. My chicken florentine.

> Not flatulence.

Haha. Um, maybe we should just order a pizza :)

WHAT'S COOKIN'

Odd Donut Shop Order

home by 12

We just started I'll play just one tourney

so how long

Two maybe three hours

ok hot gigglfarting a donut

hot chocolate and a donut

Gigglfarting?! Hahahahhahahhahahaha babababa

I dunno what the fuck gigglfarting is or why its in my phones auto correct

Send

Lunch Invite

In Treatment

Empty Fridge

Messages **Lindsey** Edit

What do you want to do for dinner? We have Mongols again

No food. Not Mongols. We do not have Mongols either

Hahaha

I don't know where that even came from

Stupid autocorrect

:)

Send

DAMN YOU, AUTOCORRECT!

102

Ahoy, Matey

Three couples coming for a fancy dinner tomorrow

Ooh nice! What are you gonna do?

Shrimp cevece then tomoto boccocini salad then roasted baby pirates with garlic

Send

Snap, Crackle, WTF?

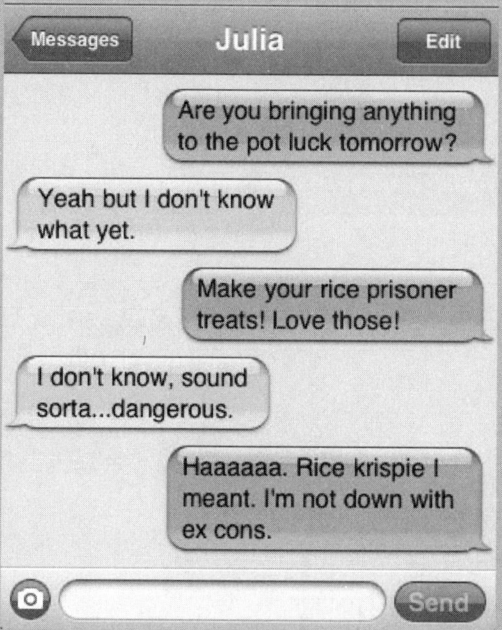

General Tso

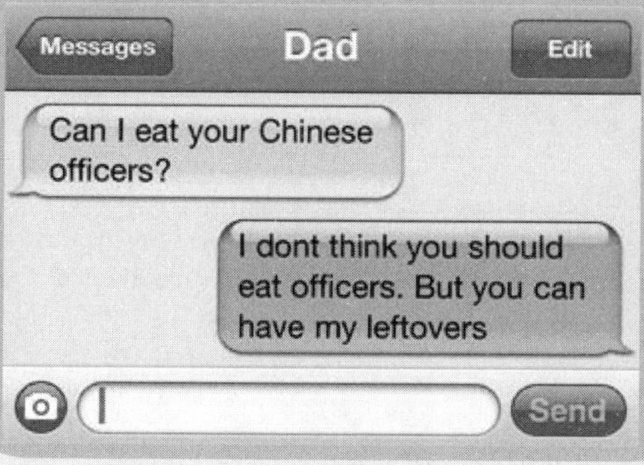

Shopping List

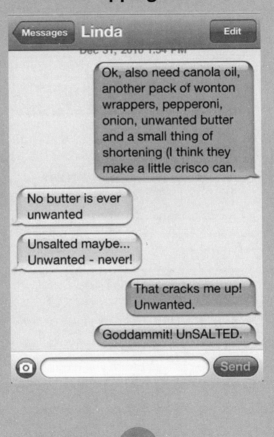

DAMN YOU, AUTOCORRECT!

Snack Time

What are you brining to the party? I'm making camel balls now. Cant wait for you to try them! They are to die for!

I donno about camel balls. Eeek!

HAAAAA! I meant "caramel bars" not balls! I wouldn't even know where to get the ingredients for "camel balls".

          Send

DAMN YOU, AUTOCORRECT!

108

Mom's Hungry

WHAT'S COOKIN'

Dinner for One

Impressed makin food for myself

what the hell is it??

Children and rice

children!????

chicken

hahahahhaahhahh!!! damn autocorrect!

Yep

Send

Deadly Dinner

Jeff is here... Can you do me a favor though? Can preheat the oven and then put the BBQ chicken pizza that is in the freezer in it?

Sure

Thanks :) I Hungryyyyy

I see pesticides pizza and red pepper pizza

Lol....I mean pesto

Ahahhahaahahah

Let's do red pepper

WHAT'S COOKIN'

How to Cook Lentils

I've cooked the soup for over the time it said & the lentils are still hard ... : (
Do you know anything about cooking lentils

hmmm...you might not have pee-soaked them, so it'll take longer to cook. make sure they're rotating in the broth, otherwise it's not hot enough. just takes a while babe : /

pre-soaked!!!! gahhhh! smart type sucks!!!

Send

No Soup for You

If You Say So . . .

Jeez no help huh? Do u eat dairy products? Eggs?

Yep. Eggs, cheese, milk. Especially cheese, lol.

I'm a cheese vibrator!

Lmao WTF!

Lmao I typed connoisseur and it thinks vibrator lmao

So much for all the bugs being out of autocorrect,

         Send

New Side Dish
Sweeping the Nation

Dad

They are having roast beef, mashed fatties, green beans, rolls, etc. Do you want me to bring some home or you want something else?

Sounds good.

But what are mashed fatties?

I meant tatties.

Taters? Lol!

Or Taters.

4

Freudian Slips:

When Autocorrect Reads Your Mind

Weekend Cookout

Cant wait for the cookout this weekend

YAY! Me too!

Lots of people coming. I'm so glad I have a big dick!

Omg! Deck!

Well, both, from what I've heard...

119

FREUDIAN SLIPS

Intriguing Offer

Weekend Plans

Any plans this weekend?

Nothing set in stone, but there's always someone to do

someTHING... WOW

Hahaha!

Oh wow lol

Let me try that again... There's always someTHING to do :)

I was gonna ask, who's in the running?

FREUDIAN SLIPS

Boob Tube

FREUDIAN SLIPS

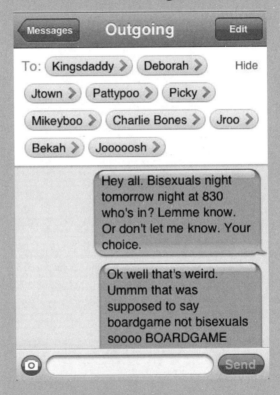

DAMN YOU, AUTOCORRECT!

Asking a Favor

Messages | Luke | **Edit**

Hey babe are you by a computer?

> Yea why?

I need you to check my Johnson

> Don't I have to do that in person babe? Haha

Hahaha I'm dying here. I meant my hotmail.

I need an email printed

> Ok I can do both ;)

Send

Such a Hassle

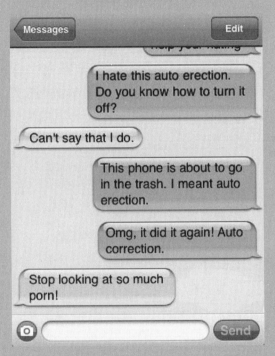

DAMN YOU, AUTOCORRECT!

Dirty Mind

shoulder? Am home alone. Bad cold and feel lousy :(

I'm ok no worries! The phallus won so I'm happy! Feel better mommy

Freudian slip. U wrote phallus instead of phillies!! What's on ur mind little girl???

Ahhh phillies! My autocorrect changed it!

Good save

FREUDIAN SLIPS

Planning the Evening

Dec 28, 2010 12:52 PM

Hi! Answer.

Haha, what time did you want to leave for the bar on nye? I know Brian has to work until 6, and I'm trying to figure out what time everyone else will be down so we have enough time to orgasm

AH!!!! Damn autocorrect! Pregame*** pregame!!!

HAHAHAHAHAHAHAHA.

FREUDIAN SLIPS

Working Up a Thirst

I am soooo thirsty. Can you buy me a huge bottle of water on your way home?

Yea. Of course. Why are you so thirsty

Way too much sodomy last night.

Please tell me that was autocorrect.

Oh. Dear. God. SODIUM!!!

Hahahahahah wow. That was bad.

Send

FREUDIAN SLIPS

Spring Break

Matt

I think i need a skimpy black and whore bikini for daytona
11:37AM, Dec 28

*white
11:37AM, Dec 28

i love that my phone auto predicts whore instead of white
11:38AM, Dec 28

We don't go swimming
11:39AM, Dec 28

Type to compose | Send

DAMN YOU, AUTOCORRECT!

132

Can I See Some ID?

Messages **Christine Joy...** Edit

Dude, it feels so empowering being able to buy alcohol. Lol.

DUI call universal?

Lol DUI. I meant did***

Send

OWN Network

Messages **Brie** Edit

im excited for the orca whale channel to premiere new years day! gonna be in front of the tv all day

You like whales that much?

no i meant the oprah winfrey channel! not orca whale. autocorrected once again!

Send

FREUDIAN SLIPS

Bromance

pick u up

I was planning on coming down tmrw night, does that work? I jus moved into a new dorm, getting settled still...

No prob sounds good homoerotic

Wow I mean to type homie... And my Phone changed that lol

Ill put on something nice for you

DAMN YOU, AUTOCORRECT!

134

Wasting the Day

Yeahhh when are we finishing the movie?

> Well I never get tired of procreating so how about in a little bit

> WOW. Procrastinating. My very own autocorrect fuck up

Whoa I don't know if I'm ready for a kid...

> Ouch. Rejection is a cold bitch.

Hahaha I couldn't resist

Send

135

FREUDIAN SLIPS

So Much Confusion

DAMN YOU, AUTOCORRECT!

FREUDIAN SLIPS

Rachael's Party

Messages **Todd** Edit

You have plans friday night?

No, why?

Do you wanna come with me to Rachael's going away party?

Sure! I'll orally come!

Its not that type of party Todd. Hahahah

Jesus! I meant I'll totally come. Damnnnnn.

DAMN YOU, AUTOCORRECT!

138

Matthew's Girlfriend

Joey

Messages
Edit

> Dude have u seen Matthews girlfriend, she is smokin

> Her body is slammin

> She's fine as hell. Matt said shes a pornographer

> Hes dating a porn star? Wha???

> Lol. Choreographer. Autocorrect.

139

FREUDIAN SLIPS

Crash and Burn

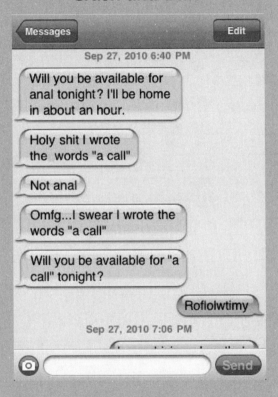

Beware of Santa

> Hahahhahaha damn I coulda looked for Santa longer!

I am about to go out. I will look for him!

> Hahaha he might attempt to rub you over.

> I mean run.

If Santa rubs me... I better get everything I want for Christmas.

> I need to stop using my phone. I fail at doing so correctly.

Send

FREUDIAN SLIPS

Two Hours

Heyyyyyy

What's up? I was just gonna call you.

Nothin! Bored. Mikes been in here making me orgasm for the past two hours.

What!?

OMGOMG I meant origami. From the book I got him for Xmas! LMFAo

Two hours? Wow impressive. If he has a brother tell him to call me.

Send

DAMN YOU, AUTOCORRECT!

142

Welcome to the Neighborhood

Elizabeth

Hey, how's everything going? I haven't talked to you since the big move!

Hey! Oh it's been great! Still getting the house set up, really busy painting and stuff.

I bet. I just love your new areola!

??? I don't remember showing them to you, lol.

OH CRAP! I meant new AREA. This phone made me sound like a perv!

FREUDIAN SLIPS

Photo Shoot

Messages — **Edit**

08/12/2010 7:00 PM

Have u sent photo yet

08/12/2010 7:42 PM

About to take one

Can u do testicle shot

WTF

Lmao. That should of read Verticle shot

A vertical testicle shot

No. Forget the testicle shot. Bloody stupid spell thing.

Ratflmao

DAMN YOU, AUTOCORRECT!

The Holidays

egg nog. Lol

Dec 5, 2010 9:21 PM

True. We can have egg nog chais though.

That sounds fantastic! :)

I'm so excited for all the testicular!

Festivities. I meant festivities.

Hahaha.... Awesome. Testicular. Me too Tues it Is.:)

Haha my bad

FREUDIAN SLIPS

Remedy for a Sore Throat

DAMN YOU, AUTOCORRECT!

Interesting Turn of Events

> Big plans tonight?

Just woke up from a nap- have a bunch of options - need to choose- u?

> Hangin in the berg-low key

> Went bi last night

Did u like?

I think u meant to say big although bi sounds pretty good too:)

◎ [＿＿＿＿＿＿＿＿＿＿] Send

Open Schedule

Movie Night

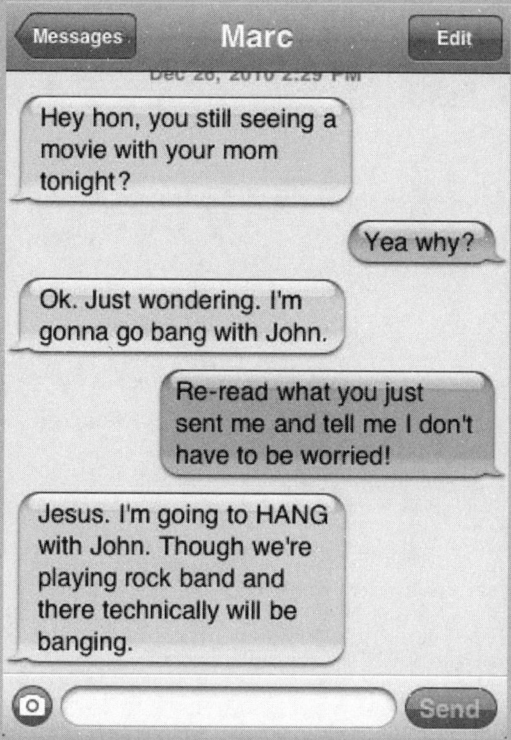
Messages
Marc
Edit
Hey hon, you still seeing a movie with your mom tonight?
Yea why?
Ok. Just wondering. I'm gonna go bang with John.
Re-read what you just sent me and tell me I don't have to be worried!
Jesus. I'm going to HANG with John. Though we're playing rock band and there technically will be banging.
Send

Can You Sense It?

Messages   **Manny**   Edit

So sure

Hahaha. I hope you can sense the orgasm through the texts.

Oh. My. God! I totally meant sarcasm!!!!! Stupid Phone spell check! I don't even know how that popped up.

Haha oh yeah

Bahaha. That was embarrassiiiiiiing.

Send

Thanks for Sharing

Messages   Edit

Are you leaving now?

I'm asexual

Crap. I mean in a sec! Mortified.

wow that's sorta personal. lmao

I will never live this down, will I.

never.

Send

Take Your Time

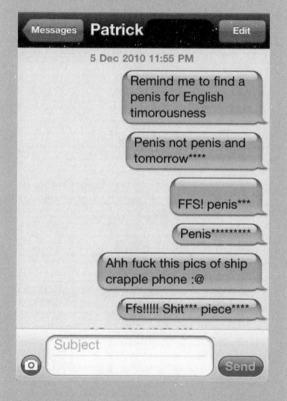

Reminders

FREUDIAN SLIPS

Dangers of Kickboxing

John wants me to take this kickboxing class with him.

I don't really want to but he's pushing me.

You totally should. It's fun and a great workout. Why don't you want to

I know but I don't wanna get him in my mouth

What sorta class is that?!

Omg *hit!!! In my mouth.

DAMN YOU, AUTOCORRECT!

5

Say What?!:

Totally Random Autocorrect Incidents

Shabaka!

Shabaka

I typed hahahahahahaha and it turned in to SHABAKA

I'm just lying on my bed laughing really hard

I can't stop saying SHABAKA

In a weird voice

He was an Egyptian pharaoh. Weird voice mandatory. SHABAKA!!!

Send

157

SAY WHAT?!

Dinosaur Infection

Minor brachiosaurus and an ear infection. Awesome.

Ugh. Bronchitis. I don't have an underaged dinosaur

Hahaha. I'm sorry you're sick, but that was an AWESOME auto-correct.

Ya. I would rather have a dinosaur.

Send

DAMN YOU, AUTOCORRECT!

Dancing Queen

I feel like dancing!

So dance

Shake what romana gave you!

Um yo mama*

Hahahha romana

Romana is wayyyyy bettttttter

Oh that Romana and her dancing skills

Lol, I can't stop laughing. I love romana so much

Send

159

SAY WHAT?!

Let's Talk About Plants, Baby

Sounds Serious

Messages **My Husband** Edit

Seances for strep

Shit.

SWABBED for strep.

Her temp is down to 101.

Ahhh, I was wondering if I needed to start meditating and trying to reach the deceased Dr. Strep

Nice.

SAY WHAT?!

Bring Your
Bunsen Burner

Greeting Fail

Messages mike **Edit**

quasiparticles dude?

English please

whasupwitchu*

What Do Bearded Vultures Have to Do with It?!

Messages Meghan **Edit**

Hey wanna go c tangled on sat plz plz

Lammergeier check my schedule

*let

WTF lammergeier

Zionism

> We're all at grandmas already. Whats your status?

Leaving in 15... Be there around Zionism.

> When the hell is that? Sounds like the end of the world.

It's a Jewish movement from the 1800s, but I meant noonish! Lol.

DAMN YOU, AUTOCORRECT!

Coach Rockne

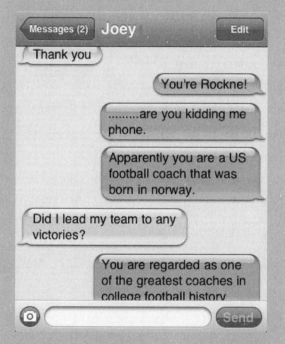

SAY WHAT?!

Periodic Table of WTF

Mom's Present

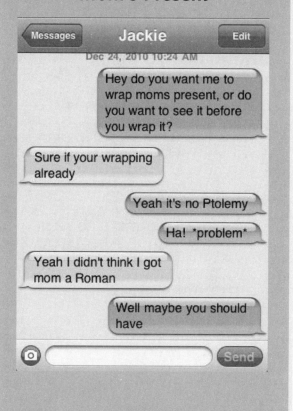

SAY WHAT?!

Fuzzy Flowers

> this is gonna be all you hear about in nerdland when the USA version drops. The books, of course, are already HUGE beardtongues.

what in the fuck?

HOW IN THE SHIT DID "BESTSELLERS" GET AUTOCORRECTED TO "BEARDTONGUES"?

> I do not know and am horrified.

BADONKADONK!

SAY WHAT?!

Don't Be a Joe Bagel

goddess Hahahahahaha

Hahaha yay I feel like a classy lady haha

Hahahahahaha classy ladies can be sexy too. Jesus I can't win with you. I didn't say hoe bag lol

No I was being serious! I know I'm not a Joe bagel

Fuck! Joe bag

Nipple tots! Hoe bag

Tits!!! Forget this phone

Hahahaha nipple tots?

Send

SAY WHAT?!

Pizza Toppings

Messages

Edit

Felinis?

Ok, what do you want?

Salad with creamy italian. Slice with neocolonialism and mushroom. Side Parmesan cheese

Wow

Neocolonialism = broccoli

I'm just going to show them that

Hahaha@ auto correct. And a diet coke

Ok be there shortly

Send

173

SAY WHAT?!

Yellow Flowering Plants

Noisy & Outspoken

> Is our lunch date still biocides?

> Wow... Is it still vociferous?

?????

> O.M.G. Is it still GOOD?

Yes

📷 ⬜⬜⬜⬜⬜⬜ Send

Autobiography

Nov 5, 2010 10:25 PM

So tell me random stuff about yourself

> Ummm okk I'm obsessed with slores.

> SHOES****

📷 ⬜⬜⬜⬜⬜⬜ Send

SAY WHAT?!

Baby, It's Cold Outside

Omg, heated mattress pad. My life will never be the same. Such magic.

Thank you thankkkkkk you

Nov 30, 2010 10:13 AM

Obama guessing that you were not cold last night?

*I'm a - not Obama.

wow none of that made sense. Stupid spell check.

Nov 30, 2010 11:14 AM

Send

176

DAMN YOU, AUTOCORRECT!

Cool Feature

‹ Messages **Kelsey** **Edit**

There's an inside pocket on this peacock!!! Awesomeee

Peacoat

Not the bird

Traffic Update

‹ Messages (3) **Traffic Update** **Edit**

SERIOUS CRASH ON SB25 AT MILE MARKER 269 SOUTH OF LA CIENEGA IN THE LEFT LANE. TRAFFIC BAKED UP AND SLOW FOR MILES

177

SAY WHAT?!

Random Russian Head Coverings

Messages **Adam** **Edit**

Looks like it will cost at least $3500. Just estimating, 4 tickets, rental car, 1 week of hotel room, food. Not to mention Olivia will be on solids then, well have to buy jars or babushka

Baby food

Yes babushka. Lol

Phone has been acting really weird lately, it doesn't suggest very good words

Nice.

Send

"Is That Really a Word?!"

Nov 30, 2010 11:47 PM

Hey it's Patrick. I got your number from Yiota.

Olefins!

Oh my god my frigging spellcheck, I meant okedoke!!!!!

I prefer olefins. How the heck do you even pronounce that?

Hahaha me too! Seriously, is that really a word? No.

 Send

SAY WHAT?!

A Family of Influence During the Bengal Renaissance (DUH!)

Out of Nowhere

Holy shit

We were working and a guy came in and said he needed to move his truck and he went out there and it was his on fire

Poor guy

How did it catch in fire?????

Horses

How sad I meant

Horses

SAY WHAT?!

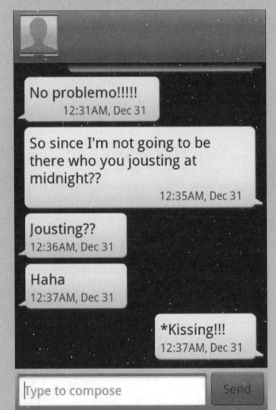

New Year's Eve

No problemo!!!!!
12:31AM, Dec 31

So since I'm not going to be there who you jousting at midnight??
12:35AM, Dec 31

Jousting??
12:36AM, Dec 31

Haha
12:37AM, Dec 31

*Kissing!!!
12:37AM, Dec 31

Type to compose — Send

Sisterly Bonding

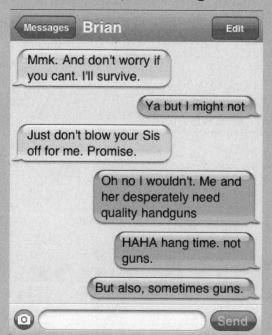

SAY WHAT?!

Stephen Hawking, Is That You?

6

**Textin'
9 to 5:**

Autocorrected
on the Clock

Lawyer Fail

Sarah M Edit

can we set up a phone call for thisafternoon?

Today isn't good. I'll be in and out of cunt all day. Tomorrow will be better.

Autocorrect. I meant court. I'm sincerely sorry.

Well this is awkward. I'll be in touch tomorrow then. Thank you.

 Send

189

TEXTIN' 9 TO 5

Mondays Are Rough

Messages **Edit**

How's ur day going?

Awful. I have a bad case of the manboobs.

Omg. The MONDAYS!!! Not manboobs. Jesus.

Haaa. That is HILARIOUS!

Send

Rise and Shine

Messages **Chris** **Edit**

2010-05-19 8:15 AM

I don't know how I'll ever have a normal job...I despise Mormons

omg omg omg omg

That's supposed to say Mormons

MORNINGS FML

Send

DAMN YOU, AUTOCORRECT!

That's a Bad Day

Messages   **Ted**   Edit

> Want to get out of here and grab lunch?

>> Yes! Let's hookup!

> I had no idea you liked me in that way. And I'm pretty sure that's workplace harassment! Hahahaha j/k

>> Agh! I wrote: let's goooo with a bunch of o's and it autocorrected.

> I understand! So, shall we get tacos or burgers before we make a baby?

 [_____] Send

Office Party

Messages Laurie Edit

Hey, is Linda coming to the office party tonight?

Yeah I'm driving her actually

Okay great. Tell her I have herpes.

Umm, okay?

Why are you telling me this?

Omg!!! I don't have herpes, I have her pies. From my sons fundraiser.

I am mortified! Sorry.

Send

193

Anger Management

Dec 28, 2010 8:52 PM

> So how did the retreat go? I was so bored when I went last year.

Yeah it was pretty dull. Thank God Dave was there. He is hilarious.

> I know! So funny. So you guys boned over the weekend eh?

Uh I'm not into dudes. That and my girlfriend would be pissed.

> I meant bonded! Sorry, my bad. Autocorrect!

Send

195

TEXTIN' 9 TO 5

Getting (a)Head in the Workplace

Call | Contact Info

Load Earlier Messages

Dec 11, 2010 6:42 PM

> So I have blown my boss twice, and it's not as bad as I thought

WTF

> What???

Look at your last text

> Lmfao!!!!!!!!!
> Nose*

Important Meeting

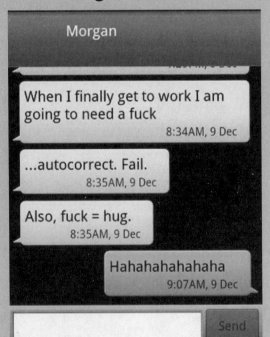

Tough Commute

Morgan

When I finally get to work I am going to need a fuck
8:34AM, 9 Dec

...autocorrect. Fail.
8:35AM, 9 Dec

Also, fuck = hug.
8:35AM, 9 Dec

Hahahahahahaha
9:07AM, 9 Dec

Send

Is That Harassment?

Is it 5 yet? I want out of here.

I know right?

By the way did you ever give Mike that boner he asked for?

I wasn't aware he wanted one from me. Hahahahah

Fuck. I wrote toner. My Phone is a perv.

And the thought of him with a boner has now ruined my appetite for dinner.

Before the Meeting

DAMN YOU, AUTOCORRECT!

Long Lunch

> Did you ever figure out how to get that macro working in excel?

Yep! Dave showered me during lunch.

> Whoa. So that's why I couldn't find you earlier. Haha.

Haha He showed me. There was no showering involved!

201

Helping Hand

Paul

How much longer is inventory going to take?

At least another 6 hours

Okay. You guys need head over there?

*help. Sorry. Autocorrect.

Lol. I understand. And no, we're all set for now.

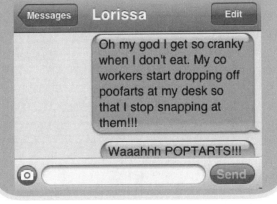

Considerate Coworkers

Lorissa

Oh my god I get so cranky when I don't eat. My co workers start dropping off poofarts at my desk so that I stop snapping at them!!!

Waaahhh POPTARTS!!!

Office Supply Cabinet

I can't find the jews to open the supply cabinet. Do you know where they are?

I don't know where the Jews are, but the keys are here on my desk!

Lol. Whoops. Autocorrect strikes again. Be there in a min.

Mazel tov!

DAMN YOU, AUTOCORRECT!

204

New Position

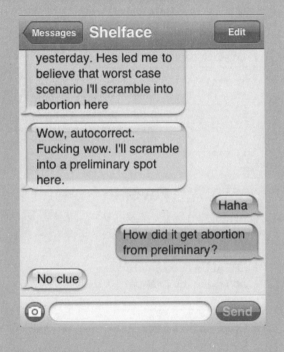

Messages **Shelface** Edit

yesterday. Hes led me to believe that worst case scenario I'll scramble into abortion here

Wow, autocorrect. Fucking wow. I'll scramble into a preliminary spot here.

Haha

How did it get abortion from preliminary?

No clue

Extra Hours

TEXTIN' 9 TO 5

Time for a Raise

Lost Promotion

Sorry you didn't get the promotion, man. It should have been you. Daniel? Really?

Yeah. Thanks, I'm pretty mad but whatever.

I'm used to erections from this place by now.

Erections? WTF phone? Rejections! That made me laugh at least.

True dat!

 Send

TEXTIN' 9 TO 5

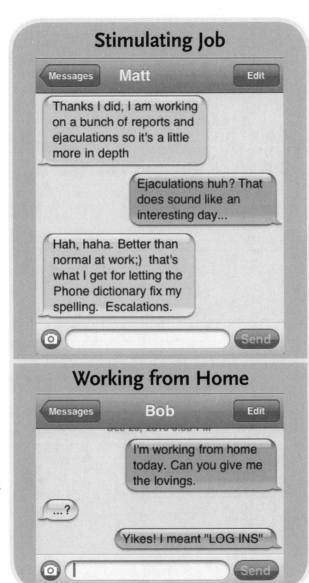

Interesting Day at Work

Good morning!

Hi, how are you at this hour of the morning?

Good....I'm conducting a sales meringue in 30 min

Meeting!

Hahaha! A sales meringue sounded far more interesting! Lol

211

Hooking Up the New Monitor

12/05 19:02

Should i hook up my new monitor through Vga or hdmi?

12/05 19:05

Hdmi. Better penis that way.

wtf. That was supposed to say picture...

Send

DAMN YOU, AUTOCORRECT!

212

Sounds Dangerous

Messages — **Melis** — Edit

Waiting waiting waiting

In Congo by myself

OMG. CONFERENCE room.

And I was just offered some fruitcake!

You really should not be in Congo by yourself. Sounds dangerous. But at least you won't go hungry.

Send

Somebody Call
Tech Support

Messages   Jason   Edit

Finally figured out dave's loin problem. It's a multidomain issue again.

Lol

Login, not loin

I didnt know we handled those types of requests.

Only on Friday afternoons

 Send

Slow Day

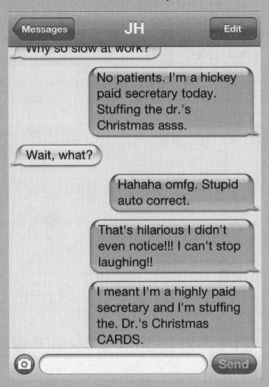

Workin' Day and Night

Aw man, you have to close and then open. That's a bummer. I'll be done by 10am Tuesday

Ahhh I know. It's okay though. I picked up a ton of shits. I'm excited for money!

Ahh shifts. Stupid autocorrect! Haha

That's gross. You shouldn't pick those up.

Its usually best if you just flush them away

Send

TEXTIN' 9 TO 5

. . . The Herb?

Early Morning Issues

Hey! Do you still have my calculator?

> Yes! Sorry! Forgot to drop it back off on your desk last night.

No prob. Can you bring it now? I can't do meth in the morning!

That's supposed to say math by the way. Awful!

> Haha. Sure. I'll be over in a sex.

> ***sec!!!

Send

219

TEXTIN' 9 TO 5

Servers Down

Hey Marcus, our servers have been down since 10. Are you coming in this afternoon at all?

Hi Liz, I can't make it there til at least 4. I'm stuck in this semen til then.

I meant seminar! Well that was awkward!

Ha. Totally. Okay I will let John know.

 Send

220

7

With Friends Like These:

When Friends Let Friends Get Autocorrected

Creepy Birthday Present

WITH FRIENDS LIKE THESE

Dogsitting

Why did your flight get delayed?

Theres some wind storm or something. Annoying. Better safe than sorry though I guess.

I know. Where's your dog? Do I need to go check on him?

No, my parrots are watching him but thanx!

Wow. I know they're smart birds, but damn. Lol

*parents lol

 Send

DAMN YOU, AUTOCORRECT!

What's That Smell?

Call   Contact Info

Yeah she just got back

Her vag smelled sooooo bad!!!!!

WAIT. WHAT!?!!

Omg! Her -bag- smelled! I am so embarrassed! I didn't go near her vag I promise.

HAHA

225

WITH FRIENDS LIKE THESE

Christmas Gifts

DAMN YOU, AUTOCORRECT!

Fitness Regime

I gained 10 lbs over the past 8 months. WTF

That's not that bad. It's prob all the beer thou

Yea I know. I have to join the gym and decay

Ew is that some gross new diet?

Hahahahahah. No? I meant defat and I got autocorrected.

I'll join w/ you. Let's decay together!

Send

WITH FRIENDS LIKE THESE

Hey, Whatever Works

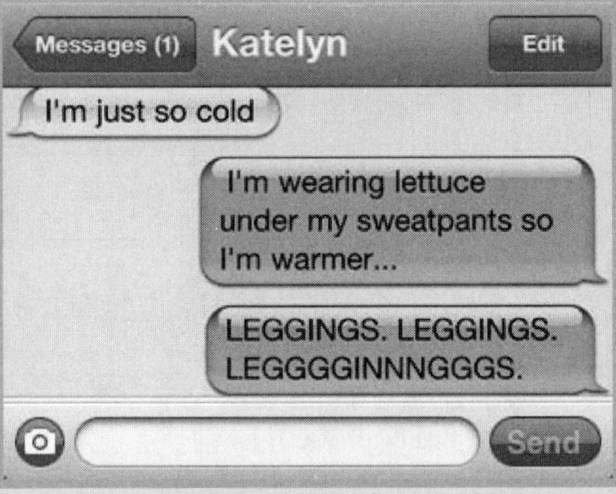

Pics or It Didn't Happen!

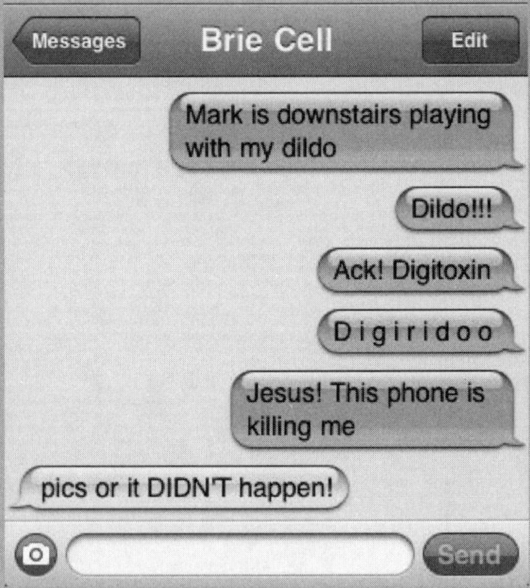

Christmas Music

WITH FRIENDS LIKE THESE

Somebody Stage an Intervention

Messages | **Wendy** | **Edit**

We're just browsing. We were looking for a crackpot for my mom.

Lol. Crackpot eh? Lmao

Didn't know kohls sold crackpots or that your mom did crack. Lmao

Lol I meant crockpot!

I know tehe

Send

WITH FRIENDS LIKE THESE

That Time of the Month

For christs sake stop leaving the bloody tampon!!!!!

What?? Where?!

Lmfao. The bloody lamp on, in the bathroom. Not the tampon. Laughing so hard. Can not breathe.

Ohhhh my godddd. I was like WTF? I have my period so I was totally mortified. Lmao

Very Presidential

Cancel   **Status Update**   Share

Going to DC- hoping to see Obama maybe I'll sneak into the whorehouse!

DAMN YOU, AUTOCORRECT!

Running Errands

WITH FRIENDS LIKE THESE

Somebody Call DCS!

They Make Toilets for That, You Know

Addi

What are you up to?

Just shitting on my bed...it feels great.

Ditying*

fining

DEFYING

SITTING DAMMIT*

Okay... Damn just asking....

that's gross btw..hahahaha

Accidental Insult

Trendy New Paint Color

Messages **Jake** Edit

> Are you done painting jason's living room yet?

Yeah just finished

> What color is it again?

It's called period red

> Dude. No. You're sick.

Holy shit. Its called Persian red! I got autocorrected. Epic fail

> Omggggg we are dying here

WITH FRIENDS LIKE THESE

Magical School

Corey

I like the school overall. Seems like a good place.

It's getting better. It has been since they instated unicorns.

Uniforms

Housekeeping

Oscar

Go on scrabble

Hold on I'm washing my blinds and accidentally inhaling a lot of florid

Coptic

Gloria

Florid

Clorox omgggg Phone auto correct

WITH FRIENDS LIKE THESE

Clothing Options

K...so I should wear a dress with sanded right

Or tahiti and shorts with LEDs

Not Tahiti...tshirts

Not lefs

I meant LEDs

I

Keds

Holy crap. Wtf are you saying??? Lmfao tahiti

DAMN YOU, AUTOCORRECT!

What's That Smell?

Messages   Edit

did the movie start yet???

Yes! Hurry up i just sharted!

WTF I meant it just started! Damn it

haaa good because I wouldn't have wanted to sit next to you. eww.

Send

Insomnia

Messages Christi **Edit**

> I still can't go to sleep. Been half awake since like 3

Awww :(

> Yeah. And even then I had restless sleep only since 12. I feel fertile.

> FUCKING AUTOCORRECT. I feel terrible.

Fertile.... lmfao!

> Yeah that was a bad one

DAMN YOU, AUTOCORRECT!

242

Uh, Get Well Soon?

Hey girl we can't make it this morning. I've got a anus infection and had to teach with it last night so I'm gonna chill with David and the boys this morning.

Hahaha!!!! Sinus infection! Haha

Gotta love auto correct!!!

Lol, we are all laughing at your post. Feel better:)

Thanks :)

 Send

WITH FRIENDS LIKE THESE

All in the Family

Hi

Working,huh?

Yea

Yuck.

Nov 13, 2010 7:57 PM

I'm playing wii at my aunts. I'm licking her ass

Thats gross

I meant. Kicking*********+

How embarrassing.

Ha

Send

DAMN YOU, AUTOCORRECT!

244

New Baby

We have a baby!!!!!!

Yay!!! How big??

7lbs 3GS

Oops

3 oz

3GS haha

He is web ready

DAMN YOU, AUTOCORRECT!

The Wizard of Autocorrect

247

Never Show Up Empty-Handed

02/02: me to tell you that its not a formal thing at all

Alright alright.. What can I bring? I hate showing up someplace without some thank you thong

........thing!!!

Would she like a thong maybe?

Yea definitely don't bring a thank you thong, she might get the wrong impression :) umm I dunno, maybe a desert or something...

Send

DAMN YOU, AUTOCORRECT!

Adopting a Dog

Dropping Hints

Becki found a watch for Dave. She is excited about it. Glad that is done with.

Very good. Becks is done.

If you are still looking for a suggestion, I would like to have a man-scarf to match my black cock.

My black COAT**, I meant coat. Damn auto correct.

I'm telling mom what you said.

Dad's Christmas Present

Dude what are you getting dad for Christmas?

Umm I got him stillbirth from Home Depot

Aw c'mon that's sick.

Oh Jesus. I meant drill bits, not stillbirth. I'm not a sicko

I'm glad you went with the drillbits.

Send

253

Happy for You

Bah, Humbug!

Dec 5, 2010 5:11 PM

Are the kids supposed to open these packages, or are they for christmas?

They can open them now. They're just something smallpox

Dammit. Not smallpox. Just regular nondiseased stuff

Well that's just horrible...and right before the holidays

I'm evil like that.

255

WITH FRIENDS LIKE THESE

Lather, Rinse, Repeat

Nov 20, 2010 9:49 AM

On the bike now. Done with weights. Ran into a friend. Talked to him for awhile.

Okay, I'm pooping in the shower

What?

OmgHahaha!!!!!! Hopping! WTF Phone???? Lol!!!

I can't stop laughing

Thank god. That freaked me out.

Send

DAMN YOU, AUTOCORRECT!

256

Sounds Like a Great Party

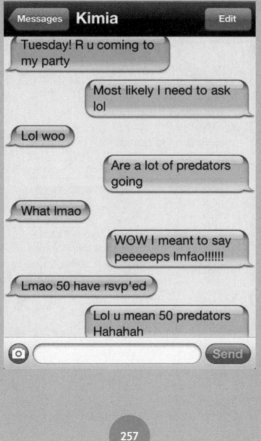

Kimia — Messages / Edit

Tuesday! R u coming to my party

Most likely I need to ask lol

Lol woo

Are a lot of predators going

What lmao

WOW I meant to say peeeeeps lmfao!!!!!!

Lmao 50 have rsvp'ed

Lol u mean 50 predators Hahahah

On the Road Again

Decorations

Day Off

Being excited that I had a day off.

Haha. I hope you were as lazy as possible.

Yep. Fell asleep in a chair for like an hour

Aww. Suck a cute old man. Haha!

I'd rather not.

Such****

○ ⬚ Send

DAMN YOU, AUTOCORRECT!

Moving Day

261

Road Rage

Messages **Matt Cell** Edit

> Traffic crap - new eta is 430

Almighty

Altitude

Danger

Blast!

What I mean is, alrighty

> Ha that's awesome. I thought you were having a mini melt down! :) we are 15 min out

262

DAMN YOU, AUTOCORRECT!

Memorable Pics of Dad

Messages Edit

> I think my sister took pics of your dads boob at the convention, should I send some to you for the facebook page?

> Booth not boob!! Stupid Phone autocorrect

Hhahahahah!!! I died for a second

> Lol oh man it always does this to me. What a pervert phone

Dont know if its right to put photos of boobs on the site

Send

WITH FRIENDS LIKE THESE

Shhh...

Messages **Dana** Edit

> Omg. I have huge news. If I tell you, you have to promise not to tell anyone.

Omg omg omg! Do tell! Don't worry, your secretion is safe with me.

 Send

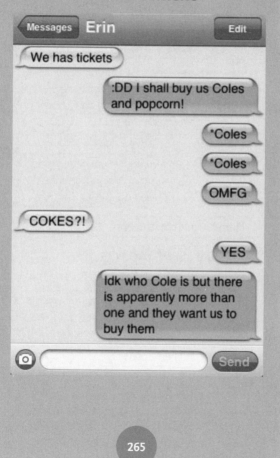

Movie Snacks

We has tickets

:DD I shall buy us Coles and popcorn!

*Coles

*Coles

OMFG

COKES?!

YES

Idk who Cole is but there is apparently more than one and they want us to buy them

Send

265

Ribbit, Ribbit

nour

> Okay, if I'm not here I will leave it on the frog porn.

> Ahhhhhhhh front porch!!!!

> Not frog porn, that is so funny. I'm going to be laughing all day.

Hahahahshhshshahaha

I'm laughing so hard right now!

> Imaging two little frogs going at it with the music blaring in the background

Send

266

Beware of Samantha's Boyfriend

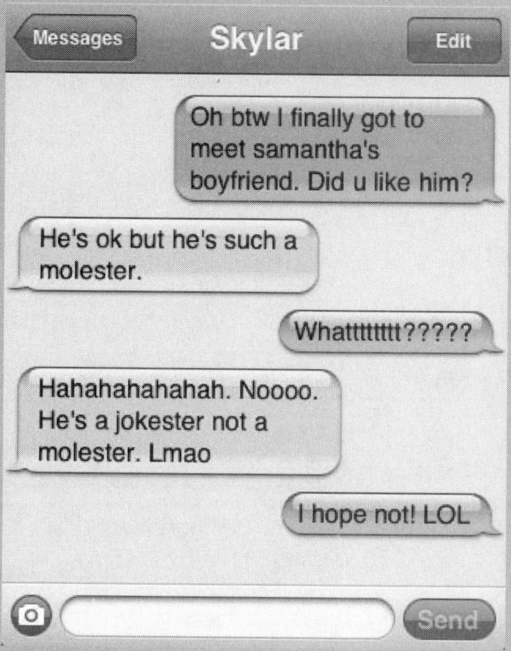

DAMN YOU, AUTOCORRECT!

Whoops

> How's she feeling?

Still very sick. HIV been keeping her in bed all day.

> OMG she has HIV?

Oh crap NO. I meant to type "I've been keeping her I'm bed all day" damn auto correct. Sorry for scaring you.

> Hahahahaha ya let's not make that mistake again. I just had a heart attack lol

WITH FRIENDS LIKE THESE

Thanks, I Think

I know huh! Awww you're so cute. :D We need to get drunkie together sometime soon!

OMG so necessary! I miss your feces!!

Ummm SERIOUSLY???????!!!!!! !!!!!! I miss your FACE! Not your feces!!!!!

Wow. I am like on overload tonight! You are killin me! Haha! I miss your face too! :P

Dec 5, 2010 10:32 PM

Tragic Christmas

Merry Christmas

Marry Christmas!!!!! : D

Are you at midnight massacre?

What is that

Lol mass

Oh that's on Christmas

Derrr

Send

WITH FRIENDS LIKE THESE

Higher Learning

Messages Edit

> I'll meet you @ 6:00? I'm taking a new fart class. Be done by 5:45.

What type of things do you do in these "FART" classes? Not sure I want to meet up after youve been there for hours! LMAO.

> Oh. My. God. ART CLASS. Renaissance Fine Art. No flatulence. I hope. See you at 6?

Send

273

WITH FRIENDS LIKE THESE

How Festive

> Heyyyyyy what are you up to

Not much. I'm just defecating outside.

> Eweww. Why? Are your toilets broken?

Lmao. No, they're fine. I'm DECORATING outside. Christmas lights.

> Ha. Good. I was starting to worry.

275

WITH FRIENDS LIKE THESE

New Puppy

Messages **Jenna** Edit

Your puppy is so cute I can't take it.

I know! I love her so much!

Does she sleep with you at night?

No, I'm still housebreaking her so I'm keeping her in the oven at night.

The oven??!!?!?! Why?

Not the oven, her cage! Haha I fail.

Bikes from Santa

Messages Jill Edit

What at you buying the kids this year? Anything big?

Gettin them all new bikes.

I told them they had to be good or Santa was going to bring them a lump of colon.

Lmao a lump of colon??

Haha. Oops. Coal. I donno how bad they'd have to be to get colon.

Send

WITH FRIENDS LIKE THESE

Afterword

TURNING OFF AUTOCORRECT
(NOT THAT YOU'D WANT TO!)

So what if you want to avoid the unfortunate fates of the texters in the book? Is there a way to turn Autocorrect off?

Yes, there is! It's an optional feature that you can elect to shut off at any time.

If you have an iPhone or iPod Touch, tap the Settings icon, then navigate to the General > Keyboard menu. If you have a Droid, go to Menu > Settings > Language & Keyboard > Device Keyboard, and uncheck Auto-replace. If all else fails, refer to the documentation that came with your device for exact directions. That said, why would you want to miss out on all the accidental hilarity! Leave it on! Just remember to proofread before you send something really bad . . . because we'll be watching!

And if you have any great texting fails, feel free to send them my way!

Find DYAC on the web: http://damnyouautocorrect.com

Submission terms and conditions: http://damnyouautocorrect.com/submission-terms-and-conditions/

Twitter: http://twitter.com/damnyouac

E-mail: submit@damnyouautocorrect.com